MW01515567

LETTERS TO MY SONG AND WORDS OF TRUTH; MY TRUE AND UNCONDITIONAL LOVE; LOVEY, GOOD GOD AND ALLELUJAH

The beauty of life is knowing that we are the light of God; Good God and Allelujah. Without life we have no hope, no future; warmth.

As the waters flow, we cannot abandon life. All life depends of water and without water we die; cannot survive; live. It matters not if that life is physical or spiritual; water is needed and we all need it.

Yes many; billions have abandoned God, and it's a shame; pity, hence humanity knows not about hell and the fire that will burn them; their spirit literally.

Michelle

I am hoping to keep this book short and sweet and I think I have done that. To you, after reading this book this may not seem like letters due to wording and format but that's okay, this is truly me. I am unorthodox hence I do things my way. This book is truly different and you will see why as you read. So truly enjoy and if you can help me to help Lovey, please truly do so. He too is in need when it comes to his needs and wants here on this earth. No, I truly do not want or need donations, but if you can help spread the knowledge of these books then truly do so. If you afford to buy them then please buy them. If you can't it is fine. He Lovey asked me for something; a home and I truly need to give this home to him so that he can begin to build with us as humans. I know billions do not belong to him and I am not concerned about the billions that do not belong to him. I am however concerned about the ones that do. It is them that need saving; his good and true people and I have to do all to save them. Yes these books are hard hitting and they make you think. So if you need saving truly save yourself and know the truth because:

"TRUTH IS EVERLASTING LIFE AND YOU CANNOT AFFORD TO NOT LIVE BY THE TRUTH. TRUTH IS OUR SAVING GRACE AND WE HAVE TO START LIVING BY THE TRUTH

IN ORDER TO LIVE; HAVE LIFE WITH LOVEY COME ON NOW.

And don't go there or think that I am like the rest who come to you in the name of God claiming this or that. Bite your tongue if you feel this way. I am not them nor will I be them. I refuse to battle the forces of evil for evil when it comes to evil. Lovey is my beloved; truth and more than unconditional love of truth and if I can help him to bring stability back to earth then I am going to do it despite me fighting with him. **I have to be concerned with him and about his well being. HIS HOME WAS TAKEN FROM HIM BY US HUMANS WITH OUR SINS. AND IF WE TRULY LOVE HIM THEN WE WOULD HELP HIM TO REGAIN HIS HOME HERE ON EARTH. EARTH NEED TO BE FULLY CLEAN, AND FOR HIM TO ASK ME FOR A MEGA MANSION AND INSISTING ON LA BUENA VIDA THEN THIS IS TRULY SOMETHING.** *So please do not think me like the rest because I am truly not Solomon or like the rest. I am Michelle that more than truly love him. When Lovey asks you for something you have to try and give it to him.* **Yes evil transferred their power to a human in 2013 AND BECAUSE OF THIS,**

LOVEY HAVE TO PROVIDE HIS PEOPLE WITH HIS ARK TO SAVE THEM BECAUSE IT IS GOING TO GET BRUTAL HERE ON EARTH FOR BILLIONS.

*Billions do not fall under the Black Banner; the banner of life thus billions cannot be saved. Lovey has to save his people; thus his Ark must come down to earth right now. So whatever you can do, please help because this Ark is needed. Many lands are going to feel it. **SO AS NOAH PREPARED HIS ARK IN THE DAYS OF OLD ACCORDING TO YOUR BOOK OF SIN AND DEATH, I HAVE TO ACQUIRE THE HOME THAT LOVEY REQUIRES NO MATTER THE COST SO THAT YOU CAN BE SAVED.** And like I said, truly do not go there because I am not your clergy, nor am I your religion or religious fanatic or lunatic; leaders. I refuse religion; all facet of religion because Lovey is truly not a religion. He is good and true life, thus he gave us the WILL and or the right to choose our own destiny. Billions did choose their own destiny; DEATH, thus billions are slated to die. Billions of you did not choose life, so you* *cannot have life. You have to and must die with death because death was your choice.*

Billions of you let other choose for you without knowing that if someone hath not life, he or she will tell you to choose death. **_THEY CANNOT GIVE YOU LIFE UNDER ANY CIRCUMSTANCES BECAUSE LIFE IS TRULY NOT IN THEM TO GIVE._**

This home is Lovey's need, and despite my failure and failures I have do my best to give it to him. So I am crying out to you and asking you for help in doing so. You don't have to help if you do not want to. This is fine by me, but if you can pass on these words please do so so that all will and can be fine for all onboard.

Like I said, I am not like the others and you would not know that because you truly do not know me. Truly get to know me because as humans we need a saving grace and like I said, it's not all that is going to be saved. Not all fall under the banner of life and if you do, fall under the banner of life, please help. I will not tell you it's your duty to help because help does not have to be financial. Some of us truly do not have it to give therefore, I am not asking for any donations like I said. And besides, I am a true product of Lovey. I truly do not want the; well I donated to you getting this house for Lovey and I am entitled to be saved bullshit. Truss mi, di day wen yu sey dat, heaven and hell will cringe because sey; mi bulldozer di house down in front of yu an gi yu di key and walk. This is why I do not want donations because I truly do not want the wrong people to get in. **<u>We are not all Lovey's children; thus you were told in Genesis the enmity and strife that was put between the two races.</u>** <u>*And Lovey did not put enmity between Satan's people and His people. Enmity and strife was already there.*</u> *And you see this here on earth. You see the dominance and control, destruction and death upon land by the wicked and evil; the sinful and deceitful of this earth. Lovey knows my temper and you know my temper if you've read some of the other books in the Michelle Jean Series of Books. Lovey doesn't have a temper like mine; an wussara wen mi malice yu, it is for more than life. So truly don't with me because I can be that dark. Don't come with your lies and bullshit because I am not giving you lies and bullshit. Come with the truth at all times and we will be more than okay. Thus I've told Lovey I truly do not want or need any strays in our good up good up home and abode. I truly do not need them unconditionally because I am not Moses that let them ride with him. Thus Europe is infested with remnants of them (Babylon) and I truly do not care* *if they call themselves gypsies or whatever. I don't want or need any Babylonian of any kind in our new world order; good and true kingdom and abode; home. Their god and gods are idols and not of you Lovey; so truly adhere to my wishes. This home; kingdom is for our good and true people only because they are the only ones that you can and must save. We are coming home to you with the truth and in truth; thus receive us in truth come on now. This has nothing to do with colour; this has to do with true and unconditional truth. They are truly not one of us no matter how they try to blend in. I will not put up with their nastiness thus I keep them the hell out and you must truly keep them out also. Life is not about death and they kept death. So because they are the children of death that keep death, let them truly go with death. Life; good and true life is the right of all but some give up their rights to death for a place in hell. So truly let these people go now. You are my beloved and more than God of unconditional truth and cleanliness; truly listen this time around because there are no repeats. **NASTY MEN HAD THEIR SAY WITH THEIR LIES AND INCEST BULLSHIT AND IT TRULY STOPS HERE; RIGHT HERE AND NOW. YOU ARE NOT THE GOD OR A GOD OF INCEST AND ALL TYPE OF NASTINESS. I KNOW BETTER THUS I ASK YOU FOR BETTER.** You keep drilling Superman* *in my head; SO TRULY HOUSE CLEAN BY RIDDING EARTH OF ALL SINS INCLUDING WICKED AND EVIL PEOPLE. CLEAN UP EARTH COME ON NOW SO THAT WE CAN BE TRULY WHOLE AGAIN. I AM PUTTING YOU TO THE TEST LOVEY; YOUR TRUE TEST.*

NOW, SINCE YOU WANT SUPERMAN TO COME INTO PLAY; LET'S THOROUGHLY CLEAN ALL OF EARTH FOR THE BETTER AND BETTER GOOD OF OUR GOOD AND TRUE PEOPLE; INCLUDING EARTH AND HER ENVIRONMENT.

No, I don't need your weakness, so truly help me like a true and good; honest and clean Superman and or Super Hero.

Strayed, but giving can be tweeting about these books, instagraming about these books, face timing and face booking about these books. Help comes in different forms and like I said, this home is truly what Lovey wants. No, I am not here to convince you of this because in truth, many of you are leery and to be honest with you, I would be too with the amount of crap we are fed by the clergy and the global ministry of God; well so called Ministry of God according to the crap humans feed us. Know that I am not a ministry nor am I a global ministry.

Will never be because Lovey is not a religion nor is He any religion for that matter.

He Lovey did not *ask me to build him or buy him a church. He requires a house; a home, a mega mansion. The CHURCH OR CHURCHES OF THE WORLD; GLOBE IS TRULY NOT THE HOUSE OR HOME THAT HE NEEDS NOR ARE THEY HIS HOME COME ON NOW. The churches of the globe are the devils domain and stomping ground; so why would Lovey want or need one for self come on now?*

If Lovey had required a church, he would have asked me for one but he didn't. He asked me for a Mega Mansion and he showed me this mansion. He was insistent on this house.

So truly do me a favour. Before you by a book and say I am going to help in doubt, go to Lovey and ask him about me and this Mega Mansion he asked of me. Truly do not take my word at face value. Truly go to him in truth and tell him of your doubts and reservations of me if you are truly not sure about me. Bug Lovey and know how he answers you. It could be in a song, a movie, a stranger saying something to you, a vision. He could show you La Buena Vida or a similar home with the same roof top and setting. Hey you could see him or someone holding my hand and smiling. You never know but just know how Lovey answers you.

Further, know your sins and try to amend them because this is truly the last of days for billions. Those that hath life will be saved, but those that hath not life cannot be saved and will not be saved. This is the reality of billions right now and no one can blame Lovey for this because we were told, **"THE WAGES OF SIN IS DEATH AND TRUTH IS LIFE EVERLASTING."** *Meaning truth cannot die and will never die because the truth is our saving grace and I've told you this already.* **Inasmuch, due to deceit of men; many, Lovey could turn the tides on death. So not because I say billions will not be saved should you give up hope. I DO NOT HAVE HE FINAL SAY IN ALL OF THIS LOVEY HAS.** *Hope is given so truly do not lose hope.* **I will not make me the final word or say. I've made Lovey the final word and say because he knows life; true and good life; honest and clean life better than me.** *Thus he's the beginning and could never be the ending because good and true life hath no end and he is good and true despite the way I am with him sometimes.*

Michelle.

Ah Lovey can we go to Mongolia and Siberia together before the end of 2015?

Can I feed the children; poor of these lands?

Can I feed Russian kids and their family?

Can I buy homes for them and put them?
Can I build homes for them?

And I am so going to stop this book here. Not *going to go any further because I truly don't know where to go with this book. Yes I began to write it in July of 2015 but did not get further than a page and a half.* Also, I do not know if this book is appropriate to put this in. See I wanted to put this information about my dream in CAGED but ended in this book and I truly don't know why.

Maybe it's because I dreamt not too long ago this morning this massive cloud. The cloud was like the one in the picture above. It was huge and I believe the cloud was over green trees but I cannot remember fully about the trees.

I also dreamt Superman again. He was on paper, newspaper. Here in Canada we have something called a Saver Bag. It has flyers in them of grocery stores+ telling you of the deals they have for the week on different products. Well Superman was on one of the flyers. In the dream, I was putting different flyers in one flyer and at the end I realized I was putting the previous weeks flyer into the one flyer. The correct flyer was on my table with a paper clip on it. I realized the error and that was when I saw Superman and I said, oh no. I could not change this because I woke up out of my sleep and now I am adding to this book.

Yesterday (October 29, 2015) I finished MY HEART TO HEART WITH LOVEY – GOD and I uploaded it to Lulu.com; purchased 4 books for which I got one free. My mind was telling me to get one book but I did not listen to my mind. I ended up getting four books for which I chastised myself. My spirit was down. ***Now Lovey is telling me that I am wrong about Superman; I made a mistake.*** What I put in MY HEART TO HEART WITH LOVEY – GOD is incorrect. I am wrong but I am so not going to argue with Lovey about Superman and I am truly not going to budge from what I said about him Superman. Superman is flawed and he's truly not all that powerful. Kryptonite is Superman's downfall; weakness and everyone knows this, so why would I go against that. Maybe he Lovey is trying to tell me that I am not weak because I said I was. Who knows, but I will not change my stance on what I wrote in my previous book to this. I truly do not need a weak God that is flawed and I know Lovey is truly not Superman because like I said, Kryptonite weakens Superman thus he is weak and flawed.

If Superman was all powerful and could do all, no sin would be here on earth because all sins would be eradicated. Earth would have no wicked and evil people on it.

Earth would be clean. Yes I know Superman stands for justice and in all he's doing; he's trying to rid the earth of all who are wicked and evil. Yes I get this, but nothing Lovey can say will change my mind about Superman.

Superman is flawed and weak in my book and it's going to stay this way. Yes we all have weaknesses but my Beloved who is Lovey cannot be weak nor can he be flawed. My ideal and concept of strength is not his ideal and concept, thus the huge difference between HIM AND ME.

I am weak sometimes yes but my beloved cannot be weak nor can my beloved be flawed. It's that simple. Yes the earth is filled with filth and there are laws and guidelines that govern this earth and the people that reside on this earth. I know this and this is why evil has time; a time limit to do whatever evil wants. Can I change this time limit? No. Once time is set in time no one can change this set time. Therefore in my world of truth and goodness; no evil can be found nor can evil get in. My free world of total peace and harmony that is filled with goodness and truth is impenetrable and Lovey knows this. I truly do not need evil in my world because I know the damage and destruction evil brings. I cannot live amongst people that truly do not know the value and goodness of a good and true life.

I truly do not need to live amongst wicked and evil people, nor do I need to see their destructive and ways.

Why the hell should I or anyone that is good and true live in a world and universe with people; wicked and evil people that cannot and will never value the sacredness of life. They know not peace so why should peace know them?

Yes we all have a purpose here on earth. You have your purpose and I have mine and evil is truly not one of them. Yes I truly love Lovey who is my Beloved more than unconditionally; it is him now that have to see this, know it and recognize it. Like I told him in my previous book; I cannot stay in an abusive relationship with him. I have to move on and live my life for me.

Family, my true family; I truly need to be happy.

I need to think of my sanity and my well being; health and financial health. I cannot keep complaining to Lovey because my complaints get me nowhere with Him. It's like you talk and talk and nothing is being done; so you have to sit down and analyze the situation. Weigh the pros and cons; good and bad.

You have to think of you and do what's truly best for you and walking away from a situation that is causing me dire pain; stress and heartache is the best thing for me. Am I lost and confused right now?

Yes I am. Heartache and pain makes you lost and confused. It kills your spirit; thus killing your life all around and I truly cannot live like this. ***If I've chosen you, do not dilly dally in helping me to get out of the situation and situations that cause me pain. Help me to help me in a positive way.***

I am building you positively, help to build me positively as well. Each one help one. You as God cannot sit on the sidelines and leave me abandoned and expect me to find my way all the time. I have no true help in the spiritual realm when it comes to males. And in truth I am not depending on anyone in the spiritual realm to help me because help was truly not ordained for me. ___I am left alone to find my___ ___mistakes and the mistakes of others.___ *I guess I am the finder in some way. Yes Lovey trust me I get it, but what about him? Why should I doubt him all the time and why should I be left broken and confused?*

My emotional state is truly important to me.

My health and well being is truly important to me.

My financial well being and strength is truly important to me.

You the seeds Lovey has and have given to me is truly important to me. I have to provide for you and if I cannot do this, what good am I to you?

Yes the good thoughts are truly there but I truly need to do. I have to accomplish goodness and greatness for you. ___Meaning, I need to prepare a___ ___good and positive future for you so that when I am___ ___gone from this earth you are not starving and or___ ___wanting and needing of anything.___ I truly need a good and clean; positive and true foundation that is more than impenetrable for you so that no sin and evil, wickedness of sin and nastiness of any kind can come in and take you from our beloved; Lovey.

I am truly happy giving.

I cherish true giving but don't take advantage and or disadvantage of me come on now. I do not do to get blessings from Lovey and Lovey knows this. Yes I want to be spoiled by him on certain occasions. I do want and need my true time with him where we can do father and daughter things. I so need this. It's like my mother, when she was alive she did the little she could with us and I tried doing little things with my children. I miss doing these little things and I miss my mother doing little things with me. Even if it's asking me what I think on something she's read.

Lovey truly know me. I've opened up to him and he's opened up to me I know, but for some strange reason ***I need more.*** I truly need more from him and maybe he just don't have that more to give me. With him Lovey I am greedy. I will not stop being greedy for him but I cannot stay in a relationship where I feel abused and broken; abandoned. No one should have to feel this way. So with him showing me Superman again means nothing to me. Superman will always be flawed and weak in my book and mind and there isn't a damned thing Lovey can do to change my mind because Superman is truly not Lovey.

If he Lovey wants me to believe he's Superman then let him try because Superman is weak and flawed in my book due to Kryptonite. My Beloved has no flaws or weakness, thus my Beloved cannot be Superman. ***My level of strength is far superior to Lovey then if he wants me to believe he's Superman come on now.*** You are God you cannot be weak. Humans are weak and flawed when it comes to the goodness and truth of life. We indulge in sin and do sinful and wicked things come on now.

Don't take me to the realm of Superman because you are truly not going to get me to give up my Beloved for a freaking joke and freak show come on now. So you can try Lovey, but all your efforts are in vain. I've told you, I am not leaving you for leaving you sake. Nor do I want or need another God. So truly don't insult me with the Superman bullshit. I've told you, I am leaving because I truly cannot take anymore suffering and pain in my life. I am lonely, financially broken; drained and I am in debt. I am emotionally broken and drained and at times I am confused. My thoughts are not sane sometimes in my book; thus no one should want or need to walk away from you in a harmful way.

My personal life with my children is truly hard and I depend on you for ALL when it comes to them. But you cannot give me ALL when it comes to them, so I truly have to step aside from them (my children) because they don't listen to good and true counsel. Not all, but the majority of them. I cannot live in a household where children do not listen nor have true ambition for self come on now. I've tried as a single mother and failed with them. I can no longer quarrel with children for their own good educationally. I am trying to help you up in life so that you can have a good and or better future; so go to school and get your education and stop being the class clown. *I AM NOT FAILING YOUR FUTURE; YOU ARE FAILING YOUR FUTURE COME ON NOW.*

YOU ARE FAILING SELF.

EVERY NEGATIVE CHOICE THAT YOU MAKE AFFECTS YOUR TOMORROW; FUTURE.

A good parent want what's best for you. Some parents to not have it financially like me, but my encouragement of you is something; positive, so truly learn to listen. I do not stop you from living your life, but I will talk to you about the negative choices you make when it comes to your education and the friends and or company you keep.

NEGATIVE FORCES TAKE AWAY FROM GOOD; YOUR GOODNESS. And no matter how I try to show you this you cannot learn; so what am I left to do? My health is failing and I cannot let you continue to kill me slowly. I have to get out of the negative environment that causes me pain and suffering and into a positive environment. This Lovey and my children cannot see. There is so much talking I can do and there is so much writing that I can do. I truly don't want or need to be stuck in an environment that I am truly not happy in.

Who the hell wants misery for the rest of their life?

We all need happiness. Happiness is good for the heart and soul come one. They say misery loves comfort but dat a lie. *IF MISERY DID LOVE COMFORT; NO WAIT, MISERY DOES LOVE COMFORT HENCE THERE IS SO MUCH MISERY HERE ON EARTH.*

Yes it's October 30 and I did dream about Tom Cruise. Not a favourable dream on his part because homosexuality surrounded him. I cannot tell you the dream but I think it involved two female lesbians but don't quote me. This dream is truly confusing so I won't put anything into it, but gayness and or homosexuality did surround the Tom Cat; Tom Cruise. Hey maybe he's going to come out as gay or bi-sexual you never know.

Was my visions being blocked?

Yes, for some strange reason. I truly could not see in the early part of the morning. It's like something was blocking me from seeing something. What I truly do not know but you could see the blockage before me. Strange but then again, I am strange in some way.

Am I dreaming about the sea again? Yes, but I can't remember if I was on a boat. So I am going to leave these vague dreams and or visions alone. My dream state is getting weird again so I truly have to leave it. Only Lovey knows but why block me though?

Oh well this is life I guess. I am missing something and whatever that something is I truly hope I find it and soon.

Oh in all my writing I neglected to tell you this. Remember how in the book of sin; your so called holy bible; it said God sent his angels into Sodom and Gomorrah to get Lot and his family out and or destroy this place.

Now from personal experience, **_I know for a fact_**
that Lovey would not send his angels into a
dirty land.

Don't get me wrong.

THE ONLY ANGELS AND OR PEOPLE THAT CAN GO INTO A DIRTY LAND IS THE DEATH ANGELS AND OR DIRTY PEOPLE.

LOVEY WILL NEVER SEND ANY OF HIS PEOPLE INTO A DIRTY LAND TO SAVE THE PEOPLE IN THAT LAND, NOR WILL HE SAVE THE LAND.

From Lovey has and have deemed your land
unclean; the people are unclean also.

This may sound contradictory to what I've written
in my earlier books and newer books, but it is truly
not. Oh Lord how do I explain this because I truly
do not know how to? Hence the spirit of
contradiction looms over and in some of these
books. Death angels and or Death then sinks
certain lands and destroy certain lands depending
on the amount of sins that is on the land. The sins

are so wicked and vile that the good that good people do is looked upon as sin. Sin dominates that land that the good that you do is not good but a sin. Thus no good can come from that land anymore and Lovey deems your land unclean. Once your land is deemed unclean by Lovey, death must come to consume and or destroy it like you see in Sodom and Gomorrah.

Lovey will never ever send his children and people; messengers in dirty lands this I know for a fact.

Remember I told you in some of my other books that I want to go to Jamaica and Lovey has and have forbidden me to go. I keep bugging him about it and no matter how I bug him; he refuses to let me go to Jamaica. ***He deemed the land unclean and it was written in the white and blue sky JamaicaF.*** So land and people are dirty and there is absolutely nothing I can do about this. Yes I want to but I can't because you cannot save people who truly do not want to be saved. Don't get me wrong. I did try but failed and if you read any of my earlier books that I talk about Jamaica in, you will see that I did try to save Jamaica. Female Death even got pissed off at me for trying.

You cannot save people who continuously sell land and people out. Nor can you save people that concede to the wish and wishes of evil all the time. Life is not valued in that land thus the murder rate is astronomical there. All manner of evil that you think of is done in that small little island. No one it seems is willing to change their dirty ways so I've stepped aside for death to do his and her work. I can no longer go against Lovey for them, nor will I put away funds for them in the future anymore. I cannot take the blessings of Lovey and give unto people that have no true love or respect for him or self. Jamaica made a pledge to Lovey and broke that pledge. So as Lovey has and have closed himself off from them, I have to do the same. So anyone that travels to Jamaica travel there at their own risk because *SIN IS ENTERED ON THEIR SIN RECORD AS BEING DISOBEDIENT. THIS I KNOW NOW.* So truly good luck to those that go there. Yes I promote the music of there, but I cannot help it because music is in my true DNA.

If Jamaican want to come back they have to truly become clean and for the amount of sin they do there, I highly doubt that because *ONCE LOVEY CLOSE YOU OFF, YOU ARE CLOSED OFF FOR LIFE AND YOU CANNOT GET BACK WITH HIM NO MATTER HOW HARD YOU TRY HERE ON EARTH.* You have absolutely no saving grace. I know the Jesus Bank, but truly good luck with that because if Jesus was Lovey's child he would have know this (that once Lovey close you off, you are closed off for life) and he would have told you this. Jesus cannot go against Lovey if he Jesus is Lovey's child, ___and I did tell you Jesus does not exist because Lovey would not sacrifice any of his children to save Death's wicked and evil own.___ Lovey cannot do this. We all should know this because Life and Death is truly not the same.

I also saw the window and door of Lovey closed to Jamaica. So for the bible to say Lovey sent his angels into Sodom and Gomorrah is a grave lie on man's part. Lovey cannot send his messengers into unclean places because Lovey truly do not deal in unclean he deals in clean. I don't know why I did not put this in some of my other books because I did talk about Sodom and Gomorrah. Maybe it wasn't the time. Thus clean must never marry unclean or go in the way of the wicked and evil; unclean. I've come to the end of what I needed to say so I think I am going to include CAGED in this book to make it two small books in one.

Ah yes what a life. Needed something different and was scrolling through the net on homes in the Cayman Islands and La Buena Vida was sold. This was the house Lovey wanted BUT GUESS WHAT; NEVER GOT FROM ME BECAUSE SOMEONE

ELSE BOUGHT IT. So his house is the Cayman Islands is so out of reach now.

No people, he dilly dallied with the help I needed to acquire this home and now look at it, someone else is enjoying it. Yes I complained about the Cayman Island not being hilly enough and too flat but if he Lovey had truly wanted this place he would have made me acquire it for him. But I guess he truly did not want it.

Am I disappointed?

In a way but not severely disappointed. There are places that I've fallen in love with truly. I am so looking at Atlanta right now. I so need to explore there but I cannot give Lovey a home in a land that Death and or Sin claim as their own due to the sins of the people in that land. Many, well all sell Sin and Satan. So I truly have to look elsewhere but where I truly do not know. Maybe Iceland or Nova Scotia but I truly do not see anything I truly like in Nova Scotia that I can say yes, this is it right now. I've seen places where I said yes this is our place Lovey but I have not seen any in Nova Scotia that screams out Lovey to me. So La Buena Vida is infinitely and indefinitely off my list because someone did acquire it and Lovey is just plum out of luck. And yes Lovey can change this.

Lovey lost his mega mansion and he can't blame anyone but him. He did not secure a safe and peaceful place for him. He can't blame me for not getting him this house either, but he can blame me for complaining about it. Maybe that's why he let it go. It wasn't suitable in my eyes for him. Not grand enough I guess and beside the Cayman Island is a British Overseen Territory and who the hell wants that come on now. He knew my concerns and how I truly do not want any linkage to Britain when it comes to our land and safe haven.

I need hills and valleys to run up and down whilst crashing into Lovey come on now.

I want Lovey to say oh no and scoop me up and carry me at his side showing his full strength. No come on people. My legs are weak and by me walking up and down HIS mountain and or hills and or valleys' will help strengthen my legs come on now. Lovey knows how I am when it comes to nature so no, I am not overly disappointed that someone else got this home and not Lovey. Life is filled with disappointment at times and this one I am truly not that disappointed. A tad disappointed but truly not that disappointed. Now we can go somewhere that has lots of fruit trees, trees, a valley or hill we can walk up and down on.

All we need will be there. Well all I need and want for Lovey will be there for us to truly enjoy.

So my search is on again.

Is Lovey disappointed he did not get his home?

I truly don't know because I feel this is like a Solomon thing of your so called holy bible.

I know I should not compare, but I have to truly wonder if I've failed him in this way and this is why he allowed the sale for someone else to buy this home. Maybe I complained to damned much and don't you dare say ya think!!!

He will let me know and in the mean time, I will keep searching for our good and true paradise; one that says perfection and truth; true peace and harmony; positive and good energy and prosperity all around. So Lovey not to worry you will have your good and true home here on earth.

Michelle Jean

Really Lovey, you are truly going to go there with me. Obviously you don't know me and my temper when truly pissed off.

Yes you are angry and upset about La Buena Vida but this is your doing as well.

I CANNOT GIVE YOU SOMETHING I DO NOT HAVE FUNDS TO GET. Yes you insisted on this house but, IF YOU DID NOT GIVE ME THE FINANCIAL TOOLS TO ACQUIRE THIS HOME FOR YOU, HOW THE HELL WAS I GOING TO DO IT?

You lost, accept your defeat because I've told you numerous times ABOUT GIVING THE PROPER TOOLS TO DO FOR YOU.

NO ONE CAN WORK WITHOUT THE PROPER TOOLS AND YOU KNOW THIS.

If I do not have the financial means to get you something I cannot get it for you and I will not mortgage myself to get it either because I am putting myself in more debt. Tell me now because you know my financial situation; that I do not have funds to keep myself going. Now tell me, how would I pay the mortgage for that home? I am not working and all I've done to help us with these books have and has failed and you know this. You are not working, so don't you dare take it out on the trees because you did not get what you want. The trees have nothing to do with this. Thus you are flawed and not just, just like humans. You have a weakness thus Superman on your part.

You insisted on something I could not get you financially and you did not help me with the necessary tools to help you get this home, so truly don't go there because hell will be here on earth and between me and you if you continue to piss me off. I will not steal for you, nor will I put myself in further debt for you. YOU ARE WRONG AND SELFISH. Yes I can be selfish and I am selfish at times but you are wrong.

I will not lie or kill to get you what you want.

I am broke therefore you are broke. If you want something in goodness and in truth you have to work hard and diligent to get it. I do the best I can when I can permitting my health and you know this; so grow up and think. *"**THOU SHALT NOT STEAL,**" and I refuse to break any of man's commandments to accommodate and satisfy you.* You want goodness for self then give true goodness. Do not set your true people up for failure then get upset when you truly do not get what you want.

Remember good and true justice, so why should I put my hat where I cannot reach it and or maintain it? Good cannot lie Lovey you know this, so give truly good and true come on now. You knew my financial limitations so truly stop lying to yourself. Come on now.

YOU FAILED THUS YOUR DISAPPOINTMENT.

GET OVER IT AND WELCOME TO THE REAL WORLD. HOW MANY TIMES HAVE I BEEN DISAPPOINTED IN LIFE AND STILL BEING DISAPPOINTED ESPECIALLY BY YOU?

I will repeat; if you truly wanted La Buena Vida you would have secured the place so that no one bought it but me. You did not do this thus you truly do not secure anything. So yes, those big food that looked like watermelon that was green in the tree I saw was you; well your disappointment. And in truth I am truly not that disappointed. I quarreled with you about Cayman because I wanted and needed something else for you. But upon saying what I said earlier; you did not have to do what you did. You are wrong and I will not give you right hence I am back for now. Do not piss me off like that because I will confront you harshly. GET OVER YOUR DEFEAT AND MOVE THE HELL ON. You had no right confusing my spirit like that come on now. I know who you are but be forewarned when it comes to my truth of you and me including the trees of this earth. Family don't screw family come on now. You want and need something, help me to get it truthfully without the complaints.

Family after writing what I wrote earlier this morning, I wanted to sleep and I did go back to sleep and not too long ago wake up again. It's after 4 in the evening and as you can see I am truly angry at Lovey; hence I've cancelled my leaving him for now yet again. Like I said, I went to sleep and woke up. Fam and people, when I woke up, I did not know where I was nor did I know what day it is. I had to go back to sleep and when I got up I knew where I was and remembered my dream of the trees being withered. It was like autumn to winter trees. It's autumn now and the trees are losing their leaves and the trees look like that but without the leaves. They looked as if they had no life and this pissed me off because I know Lovey did not like what I said earlier. ***HE LOST OUT ON SOMETHING HE INSISTED ON HAVING AND I TOLD HIM ABOUT IT.*** *I WAS NOT GLOATING THAT HE LOST THIS PLACE BECAUSE I KNOW HE TRULY WANTED IT. BUT IF HE DOES NOT GIVE ME THE NECESSARY TOOLS TO DO*

THINGS FOR HIM, HOW CAN THINGS GET DONE?

No fi real. How can things get done? It's like telling a child to tie his or her shoe lace without teaching the child how to tie a shoe lace. If I have no financial means to get you something nor am I working, how can I get you what you ask of me?

I will not turn a prostitute for you, nor will I incur more debt on my hands. I can't go into the bank and say, Mr. Bank Manager Lovey; God, wants this house give me the money to buy him his house. I can't do that. I am sure if I did that, the bank manager would call the mad house and or tell me to get out of his or her office once they find out I have no means of repaying their loan. LOVEY HAS NO CREDIT WITH MAN COME ON NOW.

What bank account does Lovey have here on earth? What?

DEATH HAS CREDIT HERE ON EARTH AND DEATH HAS A BANK ACCOUNT.

Don't say it because Death has a bank account. Every church of sin here on earth, in the universe as well as spiritual realm death owns. Death even owns some of you people so truly don't go there with me when it comes to the truth of some of you.

WHAT EVER DEATH WANTS DEATH GETS. ALL DEATH HAVE TO DO IS GO TO ANYONE OF HIS PEOPLE AND IT'S DONE BECAUSE DEATH'S PEOPLE KNOW HOW TO LIE AND SCHEME; MANIPULATE.

Humans give death power hence the judicial systems, financial institutions and corporations of this earth do all for death. Laws are created to protect the guilty whist the innocent pay; grieve.

Lovey is Lovey yes but you cannot send someone to get you something without giving them the resources they need. He is wrong in doing so.

I FAILED HIM AND HE FAILED ME. WE BOTH FAILED EACH OTHER. THUS EARTH TRULY NEEDS TO BE CLEANED AND CLEANED NOW.

As for you Lovey; you need to know that your realm; spiritual realm is truly not like human's earthly realm. It is truly not the same and when you wait until your time, you do lose out here on earth. People will not wait so long on you or for you and you've failed to recognize this. You fail to realize humans are not as patient as you; thus when you play the waiting game you will lose.

I know you cannot stand losses thus ***WAITING IN VAIN*** by Robert Nesta Marley (Bob Marley) that popped in my head early this morning. So now I am going to ***STIR IT UP*** (Robert Nesta Marley) with you because I know you are hurting that you did not get la Buena Vida. Let it go because ***FAR HORIZON*** is there and to me this home is truly beautiful. Lovey there is so much we can do with this place like acquiring the vacant piece of land beside it and build and or continue with our tropical oasis by planting fruit trees, breadfruit trees even coffee. We could put up a huge fence or wall to block our neighbours out. Look at the landscape Lovey because I see so much positive potential. Look at the master bedroom of Far Horizon and see how huge and spacious it is. This could be you and me. We can design and further build come on now. I see some grand homes in America on video and I get ideas from them. So why can we design our own paradise together forever? Come on now and ***SATISFY MY SOUL*** Robert Nesta Marley (Bob Marley). Lovey you know I truly love big and huge things. I am a grand person thus I am big and bold and truly strong and perfect in you. So let me truly provide for you and

SATISFY YOUR SOUL. Come let me feel like more than a trillion dollars and do; truly do for you because I truly do want to satisfy you my way. *Not your way because YOU ARE SO NOT OVER THE TOP LIKE ME. So come on now let me BE ALL YOUR ALRIGHTS AND MAKE YOU FEEL MORE THAN ALRIGHT.* You need perfection and if I can give you perfection my way here on earth, let me do it. So come on now, ***let me wane your disappointment. Now you know how we humans feel when you are truly not there come on now.***

I know you live in disappointment for the choices some of us humans make but it can change. You have to be there for me and you. If I am financially broken, I truly cannot help you. So rise me up financially to help you before December 2015. You see and know what I need to do, so truly give me some truly warm days in November to go out there and give out; hand out some of my books. Let me reach the right people that will help me to get where we need to be.

We need to be there for each other because I am so into you. So truly listen to Bob Marley's ***I KNOW A PLACE*** and let our place be FAR HORIZON WHERE WE CAN CARRY ONE. *SO AS I DEDICATE I KNOW A PLACE by Robert Nesta Marley (Bob Marley) to you, truly help me to help*

you so that from now on YOU WILL NOT BE
DISAPPOINTED IN ME AND OTHERS. You too
need to know about true life and if you are not true,
you will not be able to get what you want out of life.
So come on let's find our place in the sun to truly
carry on.

We need to come out of the cold so truly listen to
COMING IN FROM THE COLD by Robert Nesta
Marley (Bob Marley). I dedicate this song to you
also because you are my choice for and of life.
Please do not be sad and forsaken because when
one door is closed another is open like Bob said and
he is so right. I've found the door for you, so truly
take my and let's walk to warmth together. We
need to come out of the cold and let something else
revive us.

Lovey I am truly not sad that La Buena Vida is
gone because Far Horizon is there; so truly take my
hand and follow me to our new home. Please truly
do not dilly dally because you see what dilly
dallying on your part can do. It's not a waiting
game Lovey and I've told you this. You need to
truly do better.

Wow it's October 31, 2015 and I am so into Bob's
music all over again. Listening to ***HYPOCRITES***

and I have to say this man truly sang the right songs to get you going.

Man the world is filled with so many different people and he told you about them in his way.

Many in the world are hypocrites thus ***RAT RACE*** as sung by Robert Nesta Marley (Bob Marley). ***The system is set Lovey and we as humans cannot see the set up in the world. I know the Rat Race and I know where my destiny lies, hence I cannot forget my history thus I know your abundance of water.*** People will not comprehend this line in his song but I do. Hence I know the Water of your world and I know my destiny as I've said.

Many are looking for a place to belong Lovey but I am not looking for a place to belong because I know my place with you.

I know where I stand and no matter how I try to walk away from you, you do something for me to run right back. So please the waiting in vain on both sides must stop. I truly do not want to cry anymore. We are both under pressure but you can't be going this way and me going that way. It is not right. I told you I need stability. Now you felt pain and you know how pain truly feel like I said above. You know how I feel now. You know my pain of being disappointed all the time when it comes to these books and other things in my life.

I truly don't want me to be repeating myself over and over again with you. And truly stop with the Superman crap because I've told you above Superman is flawed and weak. A man or woman that is super is void of all flaws. They cannot be flawed or weak. ***THERE IS NO WEAKNESS IN STRENGTH LOVEY, THUS I KNOW THE DIFFERENT STRENGTHS THAT ARE OUT THERE.***

Strength cannot deplete; it grows and go up in goodness and in truth. So truly stop with convincing me about Superman because a true superman is truly not human, nor would he or she come into a planet that is plagued with evil to live like the dead; wicked and evil; sinful, come on now. Yes I know justice hence Superman is a part of the Justice League. ***SO LOVEY, IF YOU ARE SUPERMAN, LET JUSTICE; TRUE JUSTICE BE SERVED HERE ON EARTH RIGHT AWAY COME ON NOW.*** Let the wicked and evil feel their own pain of lies and deceit; wickedness. ***Good have and has been feeling it and you've felt it because***

<u>something that you truly wanted was taken from</u> ***<u>you.</u>*** It came to that with you and me Lovey and you did not like it. You know pain on a different level now, so truly do better for me and with me come on now.

You are Lovey and you are truly clean and not even you would come into this dirty planet the way it is.

You won't even let me go home because you've deemed Jamaica as unclean. So please stop with the Superman bullshit. ***<u>TRUTH CANNOT SAVE</u>*** ***<u>FILTH OR THE FILTHY COME ON NOW.</u>*** Truth have to and must save truth. You are clean, why would you want to bring unclean in your home to dirty it?

Why would you want to dirty yourself living amongst the unclean?

Thus good must always separate from evil. Good cannot cohabitate with unclean and you know this Lovey. We as humans must begin to change our dirty ways including the dirty clothing of self.

It's a new day and I am truly confused Lovey. What am I missing with Far Horizon for you to be showing me these two young black guys showing me 47 acres of land that they purchased? The land had hills and lots of green trees. It's as if in the dream they had purchased the land one day ago and they were showing me it. We were high up because they were walking on a tight rope and their feet were small; long but tall. Their feet would look something like prosthetics but they were actual feet. There were showing me around the place and you could see the tall breadfruit and coconut trees. The skin of the breadfruit looked like the skin of cantaloupes. These trees were so tall you could not reach the fruits. You would need someone to climb the trees or you would have to use a stick to get at the fruits and or food on the tree. There were chocolate trees on the property also. This one tree had one long chocolate pod on it. Walking along there were spiders, not many and you could see spiders (not big spiders but small ones) eating other insects. There were two particular small spiders that went after the two young black men that were showing me the property, but they (the young black men) managed to squash them. In the dream I wanted to buy the property but like I said, the two young men had purchased it before. So once again disappointment comes because of the green fruits on the trees with the exception of the chocolate pod; it was not green but brown I believe. So Lovey, is this your way of saying you do not like Far Horizon?

Is this your way of telling me there would be problems and disappointment and that you and or I would be walking on tight ropes?

Or is this your way of saying I will generate enemies?

Listen Lovey, La Buena Vida is gone. I know you are not accepting this because of your insistence when it comes to there. But there is absolutely nothing I can do right now to get you the property.

Why are you so insistent on this place?

I never truly liked it but then again you are the better seer and maybe there is something calming and clean that resonates well with you when it comes to this property. And no I truly do not like Royal Vista for you or for me. There's nothing soothing about this property when it comes to me. So back to the drawing board I go when it comes to you because in truth; in the living; I truly do not want to buy the 47 acres of hilly property that these young men were showing me. I see the enemies and I am a true avoider of strife. So I will patiently, no not patiently wait on you because like I said, you need to give the right tools to do for you. If I truly do not have the right tools then I cannot do for you come on now. ***So this morning please*** *stop with the La Buena Vida tirade on your part because you should have known time when it comes to humans.*

You should have known if I do not have the financial resources to get you something you will not get it. I just do not have the means to get it for you. Remember you are the one not truly helping me by opening positive doors for me to help you. *I cannot do what I truly can't and I refuse to sell my soul or go out there and lie for you to get it. I am not a Babylonian, so stop showing me them in my dream. I will not go the Babylonian route and indulge in sacrifices to please you and or get you what you want. So if this is you, then you are truly not Lovey. You are the Devil and or Satan coming to me in disguise and I resent the devil for this. Don't do bullshit like this because I fucking well won't bite.* I am not like the rest of the world and or some people that sell their soul and or spirit here on earth for fame; money and luxury. I don't have it; I just don't have it. I tried and failed Lovey, accept that. If you want someone to lie and cheat; rob and or steal to get you what you want, then fucking leave me alone and find someone else because you are truly pissing me off. I should not be arguing with you over this place. *IF THE PLACE WAS SO*

CLEAN THEN YOU SHOULD HAVE PREPARED TRUTHFULLY FOR IT. YOU SHOULD HAVE HELPED ME POSITIVELY TO GET IT FOR YOU.

The fact that I have to quarrel with you over La Buena Vida tells me that this place was truly not true for us.

THERE SHOULD BE NO QUARRELING BETWEEN ME AND YOU WHEN IT COMES TO YOUR GOOD AND TRUE BEST INTEREST. NO LAND IS WORTH ME QUARRELING WITH YOU ABOUT AND OR OVER.

Lovey, if you want this place so badly, then let someone else get it for you. I am willing to step aside as painful as it is.

I TRULY DO NOT NEED STRIFE BETWEEN ME AND YOU. YOU ARE PUTTING STRIFE THERE AND I TRULY DON'T KNOW WHY. I TRULY DON'T LIKE IT SO TRULY STOP IT.

I have no means to get this place so let someone else truly do for you because the fuss is there and you know me and fuss. I walk away from it. ***If we have to fight, then it's truly not worth it for me.*** So I am truly walking away from you with this because I truly cannot give you what I cannot and I am not going to argue with you about this daily.

I know your hurt and pain but you have to wane it like I said. I cannot help you, so truly move on to another source that can. It's only fair to you.

Fam and people maybe I am missing something but I can't battle Lovey over something I do not have the financial means to get him.

I know his insistence but what can I do if doors; good and positive doors are not being opened for me. I have to let things go and let someone else do. I cannot and will not fight with Lovey over something I truly cannot give him; nor do I have the financial resources to get him.

So yes the disappointment is there and I truly have to let go of Far Horizon. This is truly not what Lovey wants or need.

Oh, in my dreams above in the earlier part of this book, I forgot to mention about this massive storm that I saw that is to hit the Caribbean. The dream is vague and I cannot remember it fully so this one I am so going to have to watch and see.

This morning (November 1, 2015) I was dreaming about Russian strong men. It's weird because I am into strong men but wow.

Yea Mark Henry big up yuself!!!!

Like I said, I was dreaming about Russian strong men and I think it's because I was watching Racism in Russia and Mikhail Koklyaev. Man is this man ever strong; a brute when it comes to strength.

Damn!!!

I guess Russian Men you can say are build like work horses. They are work horses in the natural sense because the skinny Russian Man is strong too. I guess strength and being a power house is in their genes; DNA for real.

So wow when it comes to strength in Russia.

But with all that said, this morning, well it's still morning and I am confused with the time. My computer is saying one thing and my microwave is saying another when it comes to time. So I am not sure if it's daylight savings time for which I was expecting further on in November. Oh well, will find out as the day progresses.

So yes this morning I was talking to Lovey my way about souls and the coldness I feel and see in Russian people. I was asking Lovey if one could lose their soul not spirit but their soul being in the cold for so long.

CAN PEOPLE BE BORN WITHOUT A SOUL (WARMTH)?

This has nothing to do with evil and the devil people so truly do not get it wrong or twisted. But can someone be born without a soul; warmth?

I KNOW I'VE PROBABLY PISSED OF A NATION OF PEOPLE BUT THIS IS ME I GUESS.

I don't know but it is so weird but I find beauty in laughter and you can feel and see warmth in people, but yet I truly cannot see warmth in Russian people. Yes I am obsessed with them in a way but yet this coldness I truly cannot comprehend.

Is this coldness a facade to mask something warm inside?

I don't know but I should not generalize because some black men are blank; this cold to the tough and void of warmth.

Touch and sight is key to me, thus I have to ask again, can the cold not make you have no soul? And this soul has nothing to do with evil but has all to do with warmth; sight and feel. I look intimidating people so I know what I am talking about. But where does warmth come into life?

What light does warmth give apart from an orange and or yellow glow to some?

I know there is a cold touch but this has nothing to do with death.

Thus I have to ask, *IS WARMTH TRUE BEAUTY?*

IS COLDNESS TRUE DARKNESS?

I don't know on this day because warmth is truly important to me not cold. I am just stunned on this day people. Maybe it's me; thus warmth cannot live in the cold and the cold cannot live in the warmth if that makes any sense. Each one brings about the death of the other I guess.

Strange!

So yes life in itself can be complicated and it is complicated for me on this day. Thus my dream world is confusing and the demons that are trying to get to me; the graves of death that surrounds me.

So in all I know HEAVEN AND HELL IS SIDE BY SIDE, HENCE H2O and I am so going to leave it at that. Yes I wanted to put Caged in this book but I am so going to leave this book as is and give you Caged by itself. And yes I am truly glad this book is short, so truly enjoy it despite the confusion.

Listen, in life there are some things you truly cannot do and you have to leave it as is. For me Lovey is truly important, but if you are limited with what you can do for him it makes no sense.

Why should I have to quarrel to give him something?

Why should I have to quarrel with him for his own good?

You cannot see the limitations of someone and ask them to get you something that they have no financial means to get you. I write and what I write many of you are going to get down on me and say I am crazy and or whacked and or I need to go to the mental institution. Many will seek to hurt and kill me because of these books. I know and see my death, thus I leave wicked and evil people alone.

Yes I cuss them out and condemn them, but I truly leave them alone to their own hell. I know hell because I've seen it, been there in my visions and I live hell here on earth. So no one can tell me about hell because I know it in both realms; world.

But despite what I write, *I WILL TELL YOU TO DO ALL NOT TO GO TO HELL. THERE IS ABSOLUTELY NO WATER IN HELL JUST SPIRITUAL FIRE. THIS FIRE IS WHAT SLOWLY KILLS YOUR SPIRIT. SO STRIVE NOT FOR HELL. STRIVE FOR THE ABODE OF GOODNESS AND TRUTH; CLEANLINESS.*

YOUR TRUTHS ARE WHAT WILL SAVE YOU NOT YOUR LIES.

YOUR LIES TAKE YOU TO HELL.

ALWAYS STRIVE FOR TRUTH BECAUSE YOU WERE TOLD:

"TRUTH IS EVERLASTING LIFE."

Going back to Superman; if Lovey was truly Superman, he would truly clean house; this earth and get rid of all the evil people here on earth and he would not have any weakness like Superman.

Evil has and have dominated this earth and it's time to clean house. Yes the harvest comes and I am truly glad for it. *MAYBE NOW THERE WILL BE TRUE PEACE HERE ON EARTH SO THAT WE ALL CAN TRULY LIVE CLEAN AND TRUE; HONEST AND PURE WITHOUT ANY SIN AND EVIL WHATSOEVER.*

Life; true life is given and we are to live it good and true come on now. What does it prophet whoops profit anyone to lose their soul and or spirit to the forces of hell? Lovey gave us all life and we were to choose good and true life not death come on now. Thus your 2 H's; one you go to die and the other you go to live according to man; humans. One you cannot die to go to and the other, you must die to die and this is truly a crying shame and pity. So let me stop this book here because I truly do not want to get any further.

My beloved knows he has to do better and if he truly want and need a good and true home, he has to give the right and proper tools to the people he need to get them for him. You cannot say you want something from someone who truly do not have the resources to get it for you come on now.

We will fail and we do fail as you can truly see with me. If you do not give, how are you going to get?

Ask and you shall receive?

Ask and you shall receive truly does not work for all. Look how long I've been asking for certain things of Lovey and I truly do not receive. Like I said, Lovey has no credit here on earth and we made it so.

He Lovey needs to build truthfully for self. Man has taken all from him and promoted evil over him. Look at the internet, music videos, movies, certain books, songs, the so called holy bible of man that you read, the churches of the globe; your clergy, so called holy men, the mosques and synagogues, temples and see for yourself.

Our lives are filled with sin but yet, at the end of the day after doing all your evil, you are looking to Lovey; God for a saving grace. Lovey is truly not counted by humans but yet we want him to save us. Now tell me how does this work?

You know not Lovey but you want him to save you and give you all?

Michelle Jean

I've closed this book and now I am going to have to open it. It's November 2, 2015 and I had the weirdest dreams. I will not give you all of them but this one particular dream scared me in a sense because I truly do not know what this dream represent. Dreamt Halloween death costume; you know what let me Google search the costume I am talking about because my description will truly confuse you.

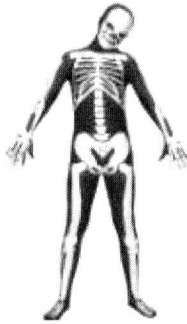

This is the best costume I could find on Google and as usual no copyright infringement intended. This picture is used for illustration only. In the dream there was no mask and you could not see the feet.

The body had feet but you could not see it from the ankle down. I was not fully penetrating the feet but you get the idea. Fam and people, I truly don't know because all I saw was a body hanging. It's like it just dropped down and the body was in a hanging position as if someone had hung the person. These bodies as in the picture above was all you could see. But it was only one that was hanging as if someone hung the person. ***THIS WAS A HATE CRIME. I KNOW THIS FOR A FACT BECAUSE AT THE END IT SAID DEATH TO WHITE AND BLACK JEWS.*** So I truly do not know if there is going to be attacks on Black and White Jews or if Light Skinned Black and or Bi-racial children and family is going to be attacked somewhere. And I am sorry people for using Light Skinned Blacks and Bi-racial because these words are so freaking negative, but I need for you to see from a society standpoint. And this is a shit explanation. You know the hell what I mean. Man this is so jacked up because I could not go back to sleep after that. Wow. Hence Lovey, please protect your true Black and White Jews including me and my family from this. ***The hate is coming with death thus let no one die because people cannot accept the truth. Take away the death from me and my family including all TRUE BLACK AND WHITE JEW BECAUSE THIS HATE IS NOT WARRANTED. YOU CHOSE US YOU DID NOT CHOOSE THEM.***

NOW THE LIVES OF OUR PEOPLE ARE IN JEOPARDY AND IT'S NOT FAIR. YOU CANNOT KILL A MAN; HUMAN FOR THE TRUTH ABOUT YOU.

YOU CANNOT LYNCH SOMEONE BECAUSE THEY DO NOT CONFORM WITH AND OR TO

YOUR UNJUST AND EVIL WAYS. SO LOVEY TRULY PROTECT US IN THE LIVING AND IN THE SPIRITUAL REALM FROM THIS TYPE OF HATE AND WICKEDNESS THAT IS COMING.

Truly return evil back to sender and let justice truly be served. I've told you, the wicked can no longer prey on the good and you are not listening. You need to truly listen. Like I said, you chose us (the Jews) as your people thus we fall under your good banner of life. I know the truth Lovey hence you show me the truth, but squash this hatred and death that is rising against our good and true people; black and white Jews. You know it's not warranted, thus evil must go from this earth because evil did not create; birth this planet, you did.

Death's people have no bleeping right to do this and this is why I keep telling you to separate your good and true people from death's people. You created this earth and despite WILL; the will of man that destroy and kill, they have no right to touch us. We are the ones keeping this planet going.

We are the ones you trust over them.

We are the ones you favour and look to.
We are the ones to carry your truth.

We are the ones to truly care and you cannot continue to abandon us and leave us with them. It's not right nor is it fair on your part. You cannot show me justice than abandon your people. This new hatred must not come to light because no more of our blood should be shed on land because of wicked and evil; sinful and deceitful demons that are hell bound literally.

We are your children and you need to be strong for us; your true people and children. I do not spread hate and strife nor do I like strife; so bleep them that want to kill us for the truth. The fact is we keep this earth going because if we were to leave, they would all die right away. ***We help to maintain and sustain this earth so that they can live and I say no more Lovey. Return death back to sender and let not death and their wicked and evil people TOUCH OUR GOOD AND TRUE PEOPLE.***

Remember your choice of life Lovey. We are your choice and you created this world, so why should wicked and evil people continue to provoke us? *THEY TRULY DON'T LIKE US THEREFORE THEY CANNOT LIKE YOU. YOU HATE THE FATHER THUS YOU HATE THE CHILD.*

YOU HATE THE CHILD THEN YOU CANNOT TRULY LOVE THE MOTHER. YOU HATE HER

__AS WELL.__ You know this is true Lovey because you truly see this with me now. This is you as well, but you leave and don't return. You cannot stand bullshit hence WE BOTH KEEP MALICE. And you cannot say I am lying because all I have to do is point to your absence here on earth.

Death's children too damn nasty, so why are you still providing for them; death's children and people?

You cannot love or truly love death's children come on now. When did unclean become your home?

Did death's children not take us from you and now we are trying to get back to you and can't because of them?

They lie to us thus keeping us away from you.

They give us filth to eat and drink whilst riding on your coattail and you let them. Why?

Lovey no now man come on now. Be fair man come on now. Why should our people die because of wicked and evil people? They don't like us but yet you allow us to continue to live amongst them when you know true love cannot live with or amongst love. Thus love and hate can never be friends. Your people which is our people cannot be friends with them. They are truly not one of us and you know this. The devil cannot be reformed, so why are you still trying with them? The time of death is done; over. Evil screwed over mankind and humankind and you know this. So let it be done by giving Death his true and evil own. Let them go.

Death and their people can no longer ride on the coattail of our good and true people; the true black race come on now. Let this be truly done because the *SOUTH TRULY DO NOT WANT TO HAVE ANYTHING TO DO WITH THE NORTH DUE TO POLAR ENERGY; NEGATIVE ENERGY AND LIES.* One seek to conquer, control and dominate and the other seek true peace and harmony; truth and cleanliness for everyone. So please Lovey, truly do something to combat this new hate and killing wave that is to come.

As for my dream with the reporter (Lloyd Robinson) Lovey, truly let goodness come out of this dream here in the physical realm.

Also thank you for letting me see my mother and talking with her.

I am so sorry I did not get to finish this book yesterday.

Maybe it was for the better because I dreamt about my mother again in the afternoon. We were at the airport and we were asking this white man about five six to five nine in height and medium built and dressed in black questions. So I am back to travelling. Yea me!!!

Dreamt my sister crying because something happened and we knew but did not tell her. She began to cry and said, why didn't you tell me this was going to happen? So I have to talk to her about her husband and daughter because this dream pertains to them.

It's November 3 now and this morning I dreamt all fighting dreams. I cannot truly remember if war broke out but you know what, I am going to leave this alone because I truly cannot remember.

Dreamt Charlize Theron in an armoured vehicle and all you could see was fighting. She had this young boy with black curly hair driving this armoured vehicle. I would say he was about 16 if not a tad older if not younger. People were trying to kill Charlize. One set of people were chasing her during the night and you could see her standing up in the armoured vehicle. She escaped unharmed. But when she got to another destination lord have mercy because all you could see was arrows coming straight at her and the vehicle. Fam and People, I have never in my life seen so many arrows being shot at one person. Wow because this was more than a heavy shower of arrows coming at her in the dream. She managed to ward all these arrows off but waiting in the wings was more people that wanted to kill her. In the dream I did not get hit by any of the arrow and I found a place where children were hiding from the crossfire and stayed with them. So, maybe there is going to be another Mad Max movie coming out soon.

Also dreamt a plane crash. This plane was different because only two people were on the flight. Two white businessman but this plane was designed differently. It was designed so that if by chance it crashed it would not crash as planes would crash if that makes any sense. There was like a round disc like underbelly that would take over and cause the plane to land. Do not think UFO but more of a zinc or aluminum panel that is circular and can retract and widen. Oh man, I know what I am talking about but can't explain it properly. Anyway, the plane came down and both gentleman came out of the plane unhurt. One of the men reminded me of Donald Trump but younger. They were in black and the plane came down in this grassy, tall grass area. When the plane came down the one that looked like Donald Trump to me but younger ran into the grass. He was looking for something and we followed him. He found this black bag and was rummaging through it. So I truly don't know. Got to watch this dream and see because I am pretty sure this is not the first time I had a dream like this one.

I've had a similar dream to this one long ago.

So in all that you do, truly take care of you and please do not mind the mistakes in this book.

Do take care until my next book.

Michelle

OTHER BOOKS BY MICHELLE JEAN

Blackman Redemption – The Fall of Michelle Jean
Blackman Redemption – After the Fall Apology
Blackman Redemption – World Cry – Christine Lewis
Blackman Redemption
Blackman Redemption – The Rise and Fall of Jamaica
Blackman Redemption – The War of Israel
Blackman Redemption – The Way I Speak to God
Blackman Redemption – A Little Talk With Man
Blackman Redemption – The Den of Thieves
Blackman Redemption – The Death of Jamaica
Blackman Redemption – Happy Mother's Day
Blackman Redemption – The Death of Faith
Blackman Redemption – The War of Religion
Blackman Redemption – The Death of Russia
Blackman Redemption – The Truth
Blackman Redemption – Spiritual War
Blackman Redemption – The Youths
Blackman Redemption – Black Man Where Is Your God?

The New Book of Life
The New Book of Life – A Cry For The Children
The New Book of Life – Judgement
The New Book of Life – Love Bound
The New Book of Life – Me
The New Book of Life – Life

Just One of Those Days
Book Two – Just One of Those Days
Just One of Those Days – Book Three The Way I Feel
Just One of Those Days – Book Four

The Days I Am Weak
Crazy Thoughts – My Book of Sin
Broken
Ode to Mr. Dean Fraser

A Little Little Talk
A Little Little Talk – Book Two

Prayers
My Collective
A Little Talk/A Time For Fun and Play
Simple Poems
Behind The Scars
Songs of Praise And Love

Love Bound
Love Bound – Book Two

Dedication Unto My Kids
More Talk
Saving America From A Woman's Perspective
My Collective the Other Side of Me
My Collective the Dark Side of Me
A Blessed Day
Lose To Win
My Doubtful Days – Book One

My Little Talk With God
My Little Talk With God – Book Two

A Different Mood and World – Thinking
My Nagging Day
My Nagging Day – Book Two

Friday September 13, 2013
My True Love
It Would Be You
My Day

A Little Advice – Talk
1313, 2032, 2132 – The End of Man
Tata

MICHELLE'S BOOK BLOG – BOOKS 1 – 22

My Problem Day
A Better Way
Stay – Adultery and the Weight of Sin – Cleanliness
Message

Let's Talk
Lonely Days – Foundation
A Little Talk With Jamaica – As Long As I Live
Instructions For Death
My Lonely Thoughts
My Lonely Thoughts – Book Two
My Morning Talks – Prayers With God
What A Mess
My Little Book
A Little Word With You
My First Trip of 2015
Black Mother – Mama Africa
Islamic Thought
My California Trip January 2015
My True Devotion by Michelle – Michelle Jean
My Many Questions To God
My Talk

My Talk Book Two
My Talk Book Three – The Rise of Michelle Jean
My Talk Book Four
My Talk Book Five
My Talk Book Six
My Talk Book Seven
My Talk Book Eight – My Depression
My Talk Book Nine – Death
My Talk Book Ten – Wow
My Day – Book Two
My Talk Book Eleven – What About December?
Haven Hill
What About December – Book Two
My Talk Book Twelve – Summary and or Confusion
My Talk Book Thirteen
My Talk Book Fourteen – My Talk With God
My Talk Book Fifteen – My Talk
My Thoughts – Freedom
My Heart to Heart With Lovey – God